Kristen Suzanne's
EASY
Raw Vegan
Smoothies,
Juices, Elixirs
& Drinks

The Definitive Raw Fooder's Book of
Beverage Recipes for Boosting Energy,
Getting Healthy, Losing Weight, Having Fun,
or Cutting Loose... *Including Wine Drinks!*

by Kristen Suzanne

*Green
Butterfly
Press*

Scottsdale, Arizona

OTHER BOOKS BY KRISTEN SUZANNE

- *Kristen's Raw: The EASY Way to Get Started & Succeed at the Raw Food Vegan Diet & Lifestyle*
- *Kristen Suzanne's EASY Raw Vegan Entrees*
- *Kristen Suzanne's EASY Raw Vegan Desserts*
- *Kristen Suzanne's EASY Raw Vegan Soups*
- *Kristen Suzanne's EASY Raw Vegan Salads & Dressings*
- *Kristen Suzanne's EASY Raw Vegan Sides & Snacks*
- *Kristen Suzanne's EASY Raw Vegan Holidays*
- *Kristen Suzanne's EASY Raw Vegan Dehydrating*
- *Kristen Suzanne's Ultimate Raw Vegan Hemp Recipes*

COMING SOON

- *Kristen Suzanne's Raw Vegan Diet for EASY Weight Loss*
- *Kristen Suzanne's Ultimate Raw Vegan Chocolate Recipes*

For details, Raw Food resources, and Kristen's free Raw Food newsletter, please visit:

KristensRaw.com

For information on excerpting, reprinting or licensing portions of this book, please write to info@greenbutterflypress.com.

Green Butterfly Press
19550 N. Gray Hawk Drive, Suite 1042
Scottsdale, AZ 85255 USA

Library of Congress Control Number: 2008943620
Library of Congress Subject Heading:
1. Cookery (Natural foods) 2. Raw foods

ISBN: 978-0-9817556-7-0
1.0

CONTENTS

CHAPTER 1

RAW BASICS

NOTE: "Raw Basics" is a brief introduction to Raw for those who are new to the subject. It is the same in all of my recipe books. If you have recently read this section in one of them, you may wish to skip to Chapter 2.

WHY RAW?

Living the Raw vegan lifestyle has made me a more effective person... in everything I do. I get to experience pure, sustainable all-day-long energy. My body is in perfect shape and I gain strength and endurance in my exercise routine with each passing day. My relationships are the best they've ever been, because I'm happy and I love myself and my life. My headaches have ceased to exist, and my skin glows with the radiance of brand new life, which is exactly how I feel. Raw vegan is the best thing that has ever happened to me.

Whatever your passion is in life (family, business, exercise, meditation, hobbies, etc.), eating Raw vegan will take it to unbelievable new heights. Raw vegan food offers you the most amazing benefits—physically, mentally, and spiritually. It is *the* ideal choice for your food consumption if you want to become the healthiest and best "you" possible. Raw vegan food is for people who want to live longer while feeling younger. It's for people who want to feel vibrant and alive, and want to enjoy life like never before. All I ever have to say to someone is, "Just try it for yourself." It will change your life. From simple to gourmet, there's always something for everyone, and it's delicious. Come into the world of Raw with me, and experience for yourself the most amazing health *ever*.

Are you ready for your new lease on life? The time is now. Let's get started!

SOME GREAT THINGS TO KNOW BEFORE DIVING INTO THESE RECIPES

Organic Food

I use organic produce and products for pretty much everything. There are very few exceptions, and that would be if the recipe called for something I just can't get organic such as jicama, young Thai coconuts, certain seasonings, or any random ingredient that my local health food store is not able to procure from an organic grower for whatever reason.

If you think organic foods are too expensive, then start in baby steps and buy a few things at a time. Realize that you're going to be spending less money in the long run on health problems as your health improves, and going organic is one way to facilitate that. I find that once people learn about the direct cause-and-effect relationship between non-organic food and illnesses such as cancer, the relatively small premium you pay for organic becomes a trivial non-issue. Your health is worth it!

Choosing organically grown foods is one of the most important choices we can make. The more people who choose organic, the lower the prices will be in the long run. Vote with your dollar! Here is something I do to help further this cause and you can, too... whenever I eat at a restaurant I always write on the bill, "I would eat here more if you served organic food." Can you imagine what would happen if we all did this?

It's essential to use organic ingredients for many reasons:

1. The health benefits – superior nutrition, reduced intake of chemicals and heavy metals and decreased exposure to carcinogens. Organic food has been shown to have up to 300% more nutrition than conventionally grown, non-organic produce.

2. To have the very best tasting food ever! I've had people tell me in my classes that they never knew vegetables tasted so good – and it's because I only use organic.

3. Greater variety of heirloom fruits and vegetables.

4. Cleaner rivers and waterways for our earth, along with minimized topsoil erosion.

Going Organic on a Budget:

Going organic on a budget is not impossible. Here are things to keep in mind that will help you afford it:

1. Buy in bulk. Ask the store you frequent if they'll give you a deal for buying certain foods by the case. (Just make sure it's a case of something that you can go through in a timely fashion so it doesn't go to waste). Consider this for bananas or greens especially if you drink lots of smoothies or green juice, like I do.

2. See if local neighbors, family or friends will share the price of getting cases of certain foods. When you do this, you can go beyond your local grocery store and contact great places (which deliver nationally) such as Boxed Greens (BoxedGreens.com) or Diamond Organics (DiamondOrganics.com). Maybe they'll extend a discount if your order goes above a certain

amount or if you get certain foods by the case. It never hurts to ask.

3. Pay attention to organic foods that are not very expensive to buy relative to the conventional prices (bananas, for example). Load up on those.

4. Be smart when picking what you buy as organic. Some conventionally grown foods have higher levels of pesticides than others. For those, go organic. Then, for foods that are not sprayed as much, you can go conventional. Avocados, for example, aren't sprayed too heavily so you could buy those as conventional. Here is a resource that keeps an updated list:

5. foodnews.org/walletguide.php

6. Buy produce that is on sale. Pay attention to which organic foods are on sale for the week and plan your menu around that. Every little bit adds up!

7. Grow your own sprouts. Load up on these for salads, soups, and smoothies. Very inexpensive. Buy the organic seeds in the bulk bins at your health food store or buy online and grow them yourself. Fun!

8. Buy organic seeds/nuts in bulk online and freeze. Nuts and seeds typically get less expensive when you order in bulk from somewhere like Sun Organic (SunOrganic.com). Take advantage of this and freeze them (they'll last the year!). Do the same with dried fruits/dates/etc. And remember, when you make a recipe that calls for expensive nuts, you can often easily replace them with a less expensive seed such as sunflower or pumpkin seeds.

9. Buy seasonally; hence, don't buy a bunch of organic berries out of season (i.e., eat more apples and bananas in the fall and winter). Also, consider buying frozen organic fruits, especially when they're on sale!

10. Be content with minimal variety. Organic spinach banana smoothies are inexpensive. So, having this most mornings for your breakfast can save you money. You can change it up for fun by adding cinnamon one day, nutmeg another, vanilla extract yet another. Another inexpensive meal or snack is a spinach apple smoothie. Throw in a date or some raisins for extra pizazz. It helps the budget when you make salads, smoothies, and soups with ingredients that tend to be less expensive such as carrots (year round), bananas (year round), zucchini and cucumbers (in the summer), etc.

Kristen Suzanne's Tip: A Note About Herbs

Hands down, fresh herbs taste the best and have the highest nutritional value. While I recommend fresh herbs whenever possible, you can substitute dried herbs if necessary. But do so in a ratio of:

3 parts fresh to 1 part dried

Dried herbs impart a more concentrated flavor, which is why you need less of them. For instance, if your recipe calls for three tablespoons of fresh basil, you'll be fine if you use one tablespoon of dried basil instead.

The Infamous Salt Question: What Kind Do I Use?

All life on earth began in the oceans, so it's no surprise that organisms' cellular fluids chemically resemble sea water. Saltwater in the ocean is "salty" due to many, many minerals, not just sodium chloride. We need these minerals, not coincidentally, in roughly the same proportion that they exist in... guess where?... the ocean! (You've just gotta love Mother Nature.)

So when preparing food, I always use sea salt, which can be found at any health food store. Better still is sea salt that was deposited into salt beds before the industrial revolution started spewing toxins into the world's waterways. My personal preference is Himalayan Crystal Salt, fine granules. It's mined high in the mountains from ancient sea-beds, has a beautiful pink color, and imparts more than 84 essential minerals into your diet. You can use either the Himalayan crystal variety or Celtic Sea Salt, but I would highly recommend sticking to at least one of these two. You can buy Himalayan crystal salt through KristensRaw.com/store.

Kristen Suzanne's Tip: Start Small with Strong Flavors

FLAVORS AND THEIR STRENGTH

There are certain flavors and ingredients that are particularly strong, such as garlic, ginger, onion, and salt. It's important to observe patience here, as these are flavors that can be loved or considered offensive, depending on who is eating the food. I know people who want the maximum amount of salt called for in a recipe and I know some who are highly sensitive to it. Therefore, to make the best possible Raw experience for you, I recommend starting on the "small end" especially with ingredients like garlic, ginger, strong savory herbs and seasonings, onions (any variety), citrus, and even salt. If I've given you a range in a recipe, for instance *1/4 - 1/2 teaspoon Himalayan crystal salt* then I recommend starting with the smaller amount, and then tasting it. If you don't love it, then add a little more of that ingredient and taste it again. Start small. It's worth the extra 60 seconds it might take you to do this. You might end up using less, saving it for the next recipe you make and voila, you're saving a little money.

Lesson #1: It's very hard to correct any flavors of excess, so start small and build.

Lesson #2: *Write it down.* When an ingredient offers a "range" for itself, write down the amount you liked best. If you use an "optional" ingredient, make a note about that as well.

One more thing to know about some strong flavors like the ones mentioned above... with Raw food, these flavors can intensify the finished product as each day passes. For example, the garlic in your soup, on the day you made it, might be perfect. On day two, it's still really great but a little stronger in flavor. And by day three, you might want to carry around your toothbrush or a little chewing gum!

HERE IS A TIP TO HELP CONTROL THIS

If you're making a recipe in advance, such as a dressing or soup that you won't be eating until the following day or even the day after that, then hold off on adding some of the strong seasonings until the day you eat it (think garlic and ginger). Or, if you're going to make the dressing or soup in advance, use less of the strong seasoning, knowing that it might intensify on its own by the time you eat it. This isn't a huge deal because it doesn't change that dramatically, but I mention it so you won't be surprised, especially when serving a favorite dish to others.

Kristen Suzanne's Tip: Doubling Recipes

More often than not, there are certain ingredients and flavors that you don't typically double in their entirety, if you're making a double or triple batch of a recipe. These are strong-flavored ingredients similar to those mentioned above (salt, garlic, ginger, herbs, seasoning, etc). A good rule of thumb is this: For a double batch, use 1.5 times the amount for certain ingredients. Taste it and see if you need the rest. For instance, if I'm making a "double batch" of soup, and the normal recipe calls for 1 tablespoon of Himalayan crystal salt, then I'll put in 1 1/2 tablespoons to start, instead of two. Then, I'll taste it and add the remaining 1/2 tablespoon, if necessary.

This same principle is not necessarily followed when dividing a recipe in half. Go ahead and simply divide in half, or by whatever amount you're making. If there is a range for a particular ingredient provided, I still recommend that you use the smaller amount of an ingredient when dividing. Taste the final product and then decide whether or not to add more.

My recipes provide a variety of yields, as you'll see below. Some recipes make 2 servings and some make 4 - 6 servings. For those of you making food for only yourself, then simply cut the recipes making 4 - 6 servings in half. Or, as I always do... I make the larger serving size and then I have enough food for a couple of meals. If a recipe yields 2 servings, I usually double it for the same reason.

Kristen Suzanne's Tip: Changing Produce

"But I made it exactly like this last time! Why doesn't it taste the same?"

Here is something you need to embrace when preparing Raw vegan food. Fresh produce can vary in its composition of water, and even flavor, to some degree. There are times I've made marinara sauce and, to me, it was the perfect level of sweetness in the finished product. Then, the next time I made it, you would have thought I added a smidge of sweetener. This is due to the fact that fresh Raw produce can have a slightly different taste from time to time when you make a recipe (only ever so slightly, so don't be alarmed). *Aahhh, here is the silver lining!* This means you'll never get bored living the Raw vegan lifestyle because your recipes can change a little in flavor from time to time, even though you followed the same recipe. Embrace this natural aspect of produce and love it for everything that it is. ☺

This is much less of an issue with cooked food. Most of the water is taken out of cooked food, so you typically get the same flavors and experience each and every time. Boring!

Kristen Suzanne's Tip: Ripeness and Storage for Your Fresh Produce

1. I never use green bell peppers because they are not "ripe." This is why so many people have a hard time digesting them (often "belching" after eating them). To truly experience the greatest health, it's important to eat fruits and vegetables at their peak ripeness. Therefore, make sure you only use red, orange, or yellow bell peppers. Store these in your refrigerator.

2. A truly ripe banana has some brown freckles or spots on the peel. This is when you're supposed to eat a banana. Store these on your countertop away from other produce, because bananas give off a gas as they ripen, which will affect the ripening process of your other produce. And, if you have a lot of bananas, split them up. This will help prevent all of your bananas from ripening at once.

3. Keep avocados on the counter until they reach ripeness (when their skin is usually brown in color and if you gently squeeze it, it "gives" just a little). At this point, you can put them in the refrigerator where they'll last up to a week longer. If you keep ripe avocados on the counter, they'll only last another couple of days. Avocados, like bananas, give off a gas as they ripen, which will affect the ripening process of your other produce. Let them ripen away from your other produce. And, if you have a lot of avocados, separate them. This will help prevent all of your avocados from ripening at once.

4. Tomatoes are best stored on your counter. Do not put them in the refrigerator or they'll get a "mealy" texture.

5. Pineapple is ripe for eating when you can gently pull a leaf out of the top of it. Therefore, test your pineapple for ripeness at the store to ensure you're buying the sweetest one possible. Just pull one of the leaves out from the top. After 3 to 4 attempts on different leaves, if you can't gently take one of them out, then move on to another pineapple.

6. Stone fruits (fruits with pits, such as peaches, plums, and nectarines), bananas and avocados all continue to ripen after being picked.

7. I have produce ripening all over my house. Sounds silly maybe, but I don't want it crowded on my kitchen countertop. I move it around and turn it over daily.

For a more complete list of produce ripening tips, check out my book, *Kristen's Raw,* available at Amazon.com.

Kristen Suzanne's Tip: Proper Dehydration Techniques

Dehydrating your Raw vegan food at a low temperature is a technique that warms and dries the food while preserving its nutritional integrity. When using a dehydrator, it is recommended that you begin the dehydrating process at a temperature of 130 - 140 degrees for about an hour. Then, lower the temperature to 105 degrees for the remaining time of dehydration. Using a high temperature such as 140 degrees, *in the initial stages of dehydration*, does not destroy the nutritional value of the food. During this initial phase, the food does the most "sweating" (releasing moisture), which cools the food. Therefore, while the temperature of the air circulating *around* the food is about 140 degrees, the food itself is much cooler. These directions apply only when using an Excalibur Dehydrator because of their Horizontal-Airflow Drying System. Furthermore, I am happy to only recommend Excalibur dehydrators because of their first-class products and customer service. For details, visit the *Raw Kitchen Essential Tools* section of my website at KristensRaw.com/store.

MY YIELD AND SERVING AMOUNTS NOTED IN THE RECIPES

Each recipe in this book shows an approximate amount that the recipe yields (the quantity it makes). I find that "one serving" to me might be considered two servings to someone else, or vice versa. Therefore, I tried to use an "average" when listing the serving amount. Don't let that stop you from eating a two-serving dish in one sitting, if it seems like the right amount for you. It simply depends on how hungry you are.

WHAT IS THE DIFFERENCE BETWEEN CHOPPED, DICED, AND MINCED?

Chop

This gives relatively uniform cuts, but doesn't need to be perfectly neat or even. You'll often be asked to chop something before putting it into a blender or food processor, which is why it doesn't have to be uniform size since it'll be getting blended or pureed.

Dice

This produces a nice cube shape, and can be different sizes, depending on which you prefer. This is great for vegetables.

Mince

This produces an even, very fine cut, typically used for fresh herbs, onions, garlic and ginger.

Julienne

This is a fancy term for long, rectangular cuts.

WHAT EQUIPMENT DO I NEED FOR MY NEW RAW FOOD KITCHEN?

I go into much more detail regarding the perfect setup for your Raw vegan kitchen in my book, *Kristen's Raw,* which is a must read for anybody who wants to learn the easy ways to succeed with living the Raw vegan lifestyle. Here are the main pieces of equipment you'll want to get you going:

1. An excellent chef's knife (6 - 8 inches in length – non-serrated). Of everything you do with Raw food, you'll be chopping and cutting the most, so invest in a great knife. This truly makes doing all the chopping really fun!

2. Blender

3. Food Processor (get a 7 or 10-cup or more)

4. Juicer

5. Spiralizer or Turning Slicer

6. Dehydrator – Excalibur® is the best company by far and is available at KristensRaw.com

7. Salad spinner

8. Other knives (paring, serrated)

For links to online retailers that sell my favorite kitchen tools and foods, visit KristensRaw.com/store.

SOAKING AND DEHYDRATING NUTS AND SEEDS

This is an important topic. When using nuts and seeds in Raw vegan foods, you'll find that recipes sometimes call for them to be "soaked" or "soaked and dehydrated." Here is the low-down on the importance and the difference between the two.

Why should you soak your nuts and seeds?

Most nuts and seeds come packed by Mother Nature with enzyme inhibitors, rendering them harder to digest. These inhibitors essentially shut down the nuts' and seeds' metabolic activity, rendering them dormant—for as long as they need to be—until they detect a moisture-rich environment that's suitable for germination (e.g., rain). By soaking your nuts and seeds, you trick the nuts into "waking up," shutting off the inhibitors so that the enzymes can become active. This greatly enhances the nuts' digestibility for you and is highly recommended if you want to experience Raw vegan food in the healthiest way possible.

Even though you'll want to soak the nuts to activate their enzymes, before using them, you'll need to re-dry them and grind them down anywhere from coarse to fine (into a powder almost like flour), depending on the recipe. To dry them, you'll need a dehydrator. (If you don't own a dehydrator yet, then, if a recipe calls for "soaked and dehydrated," just skip the soaking part; you can use the nuts or seeds in the dry form that you bought them).

Drying your nuts (but not yet grinding them) is a great thing to do before storing them in the freezer or refrigerator (preferably in glass mason jars). They will last a long time and you'll always have them on hand, ready to use.

In my recipes, always use nuts and seeds that are "soaked and dehydrated" (that is, *dry*) unless otherwise stated as "soaked" (wet).

Some nuts and seeds don't have to follow the enzyme inhibitor rule; therefore, they don't need to be soaked. These are:

- Macadamia nuts
- Brazil nuts
- Pine nuts
- Hemp seeds
- Most cashews

An additional note... there are times when the recipe will call for soaking, even though it's for a type of nut or seed without enzyme inhibitors, such as Brazil nuts. The logic behind this is to help *soften* the nuts so they blend into a smoother texture, especially if you don't have a high-powered blender. This is helpful when making nut milks, soups and sauces.

Instructions for "Soaking" and "Soaking and Dehydrating" Nuts

"Soaking"

The general rule to follow: Any nuts or seeds that require soaking can be soaked overnight (6 - 10 hours). Put the required amount of nuts or seeds into a bowl and add enough water to cover by about an inch or so. Set them on your counter overnight. The following morning, or 6 - 10 hours after you soaked them, drain and rinse them. They are now ready to eat or use in a recipe. At this point, they need to be refrigerated in an airtight container (preferably a glass mason jar) and they'll have a shelf life of about 3 days maximum. Only soak the amount you're going to need or eat, unless you plan on dehydrating them right away.

A note about flax seeds and chia seeds... these don't need to be soaked if your recipe calls for grinding them into a powder. Some recipes will call to soak the seeds in their "whole-seed" form, before making crackers and bread, because they create a very gelatinous and binding texture when soaked. You can soak flax or chia seeds in a ratio of one-part seeds to two-parts water, and they can be soaked for as short as 1 hour and up to 12 hours. At this point, they are ready to use (don't drain them). Personally, when I use flax seeds, I usually grind them and don't soak them. It's hard for your body to digest "whole" flax seeds, even if they are soaked. It's much easier for your body to assimilate the nutrients when they're ground to a flax meal.

"Soaking and Dehydrating"

Follow the same directions for soaking. Then, after draining and rinsing the nuts, spread them out on a mesh dehydrator sheet and dehydrate them at 140 degrees for one hour. Lower the temperature to 105 degrees and dehydrate them until they're completely dry, which can take up to 24 hours.

Please note, all nuts and seeds called for in my recipes will always be "Raw and Organic" and "Soaked and Dehydrated" unless the recipe calls for soaking.

ALMOND PULP

Some of my recipes call for "almond pulp," which is really easy to make. After making your fresh almond milk (see *Nut Milk* recipe, p. 25) and straining it through a "nut milk bag," (available at NaturalZing.com or you can use a paint strainer bag from the hardware store – much cheaper), you will find a nice, soft pulp inside the bag. Turn the bag inside out and flatten the pulp out onto a paraflex dehydrator sheet with a spatula or your hand. Dehydrate the pulp at 140 degrees for one hour, then lower the temperature to 105 degrees and continue dehydrating until the almond pulp is dry (up to 24 hours). Break the pulp into chunks and store in the freezer until you're ready to use it. Before using the almond pulp, grind it into a flour in your blender or food processor.

SOY LECITHIN

Some recipes (desserts, in particular) will call for soy lecithin, which is extracted from soybean oil. This optional ingredient is not Raw. If you use soy lecithin, I highly recommend using a brand that is "non-GMO," meaning it was processed without any genetically modified ingredients (a great brand is Health Alliance®). Soy lecithin helps your dessert (cheesecake, for example) maintain a firmer texture.

That said, it's certainly not necessary. If an amount isn't suggested, a good rule of thumb is to use 1 teaspoon per 1 cup total recipe volume.

ICE CREAM FLAVORINGS

When making Raw vegan ice cream, it's better to use alcohol-free extracts so they freeze better.

SWEETENERS

The following is a list of sweeteners that you might see used in my recipes. It's important to know that the healthiest sweeteners are fresh whole fruits, including fresh dates. That said, dates sometimes compromise texture in recipes. As a chef, I look for great texture, and as a health food advocate, I lean towards fresh dates. But as a consultant helping people embrace a Raw vegan lifestyle, I'm also supportive of helping them transition, which sometimes means using raw agave nectar, or some other easy-to-use sweetener that might not have the healthiest ranking in the Raw food world, but is still much healthier than most sweeteners used in the Standard American Diet.

Most of my recipes can use pitted dates in place of raw agave nectar. There is some debate among Raw food enthusiasts as to whether agave nectar is Raw. The company I use (Madhava®) claims to be Raw and says they do not heat their Raw agave nectar above 118 degrees. If however, you still want to eat the healthiest of sweeteners, then bypass the raw agave nectar and use pitted dates. In most recipes, you can simply substitute 1 - 2 pitted dates for 1 tablespoon of raw agave nectar. Dates won't give you a super creamy texture, but the texture can be improved by making a "date paste" (pureeing pitted and soaked dates – with their soak water, plus some additional water, if necessary – in a food processor fitted with the "S" blade). This, of course, takes a little extra time.

If using raw agave nectar is easier and faster for you, then go ahead and use it; just be sure to buy the Raw version that says they don't heat the agave above 118 degrees (see KristensRaw.com/store for links to this product). And, again, if you're looking to go as far as you can on the spectrum of health, then I recommend using pitted dates. Most of my recipes say raw agave nectar because that is most convenient for people.

Agave Nectar

There are a variety of agave nectars on the market, but again, not all of them are Raw. Make sure it is labeled "Raw" on the bottle *as well as claiming that it isn't processed above 118 degrees*. Just because the label says "Raw" does not necessarily mean it is so... do a double check and make sure it also claims not to be heated above the 118 degrees cut-off. Agave nectar is noteworthy for having a low glycemic index.

Dates

Dates are probably the healthiest of sweeteners, because they're a fresh whole food. Fresh organic dates are filled with nutrition, including calcium and magnesium. I like to call dates, "Nature's Candy."

Feel free to use dates instead of agave or honey in Raw vegan recipes. If a recipe calls for 1/2 cup of raw agave, then you can substitute with approximately 1/2 cup of pitted dates. You can also make your own date sugar by dehydrating pitted dates and then grinding them down. This is a great alternative to Rapadura®.

Honey

Most honey is technically raw, but it is not vegan by most definitions of "vegan" because it is produced by animals, who therefore are at risk of being mistreated. While honey does not have the health risks associated with animal byproducts such as eggs or dairy, it can spike the body's natural sugar levels. Agave nectar has a lower, healthier glycemic index and can replace any recipe you find that calls for honey, in a 1 to 1 ratio.

Maple Syrup

Maple syrup is made from boiled sap of the maple tree. It is not considered Raw, but some people still use it as a sweetener in certain dishes.

Rapadura®

This is a dried sugarcane juice, and it's not Raw. It is, however, an unrefined and unbleached organic whole-cane sugar. It imparts a nice deep sweetness to your recipes, even if you only use a little. Feel free to omit it if you'd like to adhere to a strictly Raw program. You can substitute Rapadura with home-made date sugar (see Dates above).

Stevia

This is from the leaf of the stevia plant. It has a sweet taste and doesn't elevate blood sugar levels. It's very sweet, so you'll want to use much less stevia than you would any other sweetener. My mom actually grows her own stevia. It's a great addition in fresh smoothies, for example, to add some sweetness without the calories. You can use the white powdered or liquid version from the store, but these are not Raw. When possible, the best way to have stevia is grow it yourself.

Yacon Syrup

This sweetener has a low glycemic index, making it very attractive to some people. It has a molasses-type flavor that is nice and rich. You can replace raw agave with this sweetener in my recipes, but make sure to get the Raw variety, available at NaturalZing.com. They offer a few different yacon syrups, including one in particular that is not heat-treated. Be sure to choose that one.

SUN-DRIED TOMATOES

By far, the best sun-dried tomatoes are those you make yourself with a dehydrator. If you don't have a dehydrator, make sure you buy the "dry" sun-dried tomatoes, usually found in the bulk section of your health food market. Don't buy the kind that are packed in a jar of oil.

Also... don't buy sun-dried tomatoes if they're really dark (almost black) because these just don't taste as good. Again, I recommend making them yourself if you truly want the freshest flavor possible. It's really fun to do!

EATING WITH YOUR EYES

Most of us, if not all, naturally eat with our eyes before taking a bite of food. So, do yourself a favor and make your eating experience the best ever with the help of a simple, gorgeous presentation. Think of it this way, with real estate, it's always *location, location, location*, right? Well, with food, it's always *presentation, presentation, presentation.*

Luckily, Raw food does this on its own with all of its naturally vibrant and bright colors. But I take it even one step farther—I use my best dishes when I eat. I use my beautiful wine glasses for my smoothies and juices. I use my fancy goblets for many of my desserts. Why? Because I'm worth it. And, so are you! Don't save your good china just for company. Believe me, you'll notice the difference. Eating well is an attitude, and when you take care of yourself, your body will respond in kind.

ONLINE RESOURCES FOR GREAT PRODUCTS

For a complete and detailed list of my favorite kitchen tools, products, and various foods (all available online), please visit: KristensRaw.com/store.

BOOK RECOMMENDATIONS

I highly recommend reading the following life-changing books.

- *Diet for a New America*, by John Robbins
- *The Food Revolution*, by John Robbins
- *The China Study*, by T. Colin Campbell
- *Skinny Bitch*, by Rory Freedman

MEASUREMENT CONVERSIONS

1 tablespoon = 3 teaspoons

1 ounce = 2 tablespoons

1/4 cup = 4 tablespoons

1/3 cup = 5 1/3 tablespoons

1 cup

= 8 ounces

= 16 tablespoons

= 1/2 pint

1/2 quart

= 1 pint

= 2 cups

1 gallon

= 4 quarts

= 8 pints

= 16 cups

= 128 ounces

BASIC RECIPES TO KNOW

Nourishing Rejuvelac

Yield 1 gallon

Rejuvelac is a cheesy-tasting liquid that is rich in enzymes and healthy flora to support a healthy intestine and digestion.

Get comfortable making this super easy recipe because its use goes beyond just drinking it between meals.

1 cup soft wheat berries, rye berries, or a mixture
water

Place the wheat berries in a half-gallon jar and fill the jar with water. Screw the lid on the jar and soak the wheat berries overnight(10 - 12 hours) on your counter. The next morning, drain and rinse them. Sprout the wheat berries for 2 days, draining and rinsing 1 - 2 times a day.

Then, fill the jar with purified water and screw on the lid, or cover with cheesecloth secured with a rubber band. Allow to ferment for 24 - 36 hours, or until the desired tartness is achieved. It should have a cheesy, almost tart/lemony flavor and scent.

Strain your rejuvelac into another glass jar and store in the refrigerator for up to 5 - 7 days. For a second batch using the same sprouted wheat berries, fill the same jar of already sprouted berries with water again, and allow to ferment for 24 hours. Strain off the rejuvelac as you did the time before this. You can do this process yet again, noting that each time the rejuvelac gets a little weaker in flavor.

Enjoy 1/4 - 1 cup of *Nourishing Rejuvelac* first thing in the morning and/or between meals. It's best to start with a small amount and work your way up as your body adjusts.

Suggestion:

- For extra nutrition and incredible flavor, *Nourishing Rejuvelac* can be used in various recipes such as Raw vegan cheeses, desserts, smoothies, soups, dressings and more. Simply use it in place of the water required by the recipe.

Crème Fraiche

Yield approximately 2 cups

    1 cup cashews, soaked 1 hour, drained, and rinsed
    1/4 - 1/2 cup *Nourishing Rejuvelac* (see p. 23)
    1 - 2 tablespoons raw agave nectar

Blend the ingredients until smooth. Store in an airtight glass mason jar for up to 5 days. This freezes well, so feel free to make a double batch for future use.

Nut/Seed Milk (regular)

Yield 4 - 5 cups

The creamiest nut/seed milk traditionally comes from hemp seeds, cashews, pine nuts, Brazil nuts or macadamia nuts, although I'm also a huge fan of milks made from walnuts, pecans, hazelnuts, almonds, sesame seeds, and others.

This recipe does not include a sweetener, but when I'm in the mood for a little sweetness, I add a couple of pitted dates or a squirt of raw agave nectar. Yum!

    1 1/2 cups nuts, soaked 6 - 12 hours, drained and rinsed
    3 1/4 cups water
    pinch Himalayan crystal salt, optional

Blend the ingredients until smooth and deliciously creamy. For an even *extra creamy* texture, strain your nut/seed milk through a nut milk bag.

Sweet Nut/Seed Cream (thick)

Yield 2 - 3 cups

> 1 cup nuts or seeds, soaked 6 - 8 hours, drained and rinsed
>
> 1 - 1 1/2 cups water, more if needed
>
> 2 - 3 tablespoons raw agave nectar or 2 - 3 dates, pitted
>
> 1/2 teaspoon vanilla extract, optional

Blend all of the ingredients until smooth.

Raw Mustard

Yield approximately 1 1/2 - 2 cups

> 1 - 2 tablespoons yellow mustard seeds (depending on how "hot" you want it), soaked 1 - 2 hours
>
> 1 1/2 cups extra virgin olive oil or hemp oil
>
> 1 1/2 tablespoons dry mustard powder
>
> 2 tablespoons apple cider vinegar
>
> 2 tablespoons fresh lemon juice
>
> 3 dates, pitted and soaked 30-minutes, drained
>
> 1/2 cup raw agave nectar
>
> 1 teaspoon Himalayan crystal salt
>
> pinch turmeric

Blend all of the ingredients together until smooth. It might be very thick, so if you want, add some water or oil to help thin it out. Adding more oil will help reduce the "heat" if it's too spicy for your taste.

Variation:

- *Honey Mustard Version:* Add another 1/3 cup raw agave nectar (or more, depending on how sweet you want it)

My Basic Raw Mayonnaise

Yield about 2 1/2 cups

People tell me all the time how much they like this recipe.

1 cup cashews, soaked 1 - 2 hours, drained

1/2 teaspoon paprika

2 cloves garlic

1 teaspoon onion powder

3 tablespoons fresh lemon juice

1/4 cup extra virgin olive oil or hemp oil

2 tablespoons parsley, chopped

2 tablespoons water, if needed

Blend all of the ingredients, except the parsley, until creamy. Pulse in the parsley. *My Basic Raw Mayonnaise* will stay fresh for up to one week in the refrigerator.

CHAPTER 2

SMOOTHIES

PHOTOS OF RECIPES AVAILABLE AT:

KristensRaw.com/photos

The following beverages made from recipes in this book have been photographed. See KristensRaw.com/photos for pretty pictures of:

- Earthbound Brazil Nut Milk
- Citrus Zing Elixir
- Raw Fruit Water Elixir
- Sassy Strawberry Aperitif
- Green Machine Plant Blood
- Dazzling Daylight Flower Smoothie
- Spicy Sunrise Smoothie
- Strawberry Banana Jump-Start (see cover)
- Old Faithful Smoothie (see cover)

I always like to get feedback on my photographs! (In addition to hearing your stories about my recipes too!) If you visit the site, please let me know your favorites by writing to me at:

Kristen@KristensRaw.com

EASY, HIGH ENERGY NUTRITION

I love fresh organic smoothies because they can serve so many different purposes. Smoothies in the morning, smoothies in the evening, smoothies before or after a workout, smoothies in the middle of the night. Smoothies here, smoothies there, smoothies everywhere. See? Smoothies can serve many purposes. I love them.

Smoothies make a high energy, extra healthy, and super fast breakfast, lunch, dinner, dessert, or snack. They can be a complete meal replacement...just make sure you make enough to fill you up, or they can complement a meal.

Smoothies can be great for helping you kick cravings for unhealthy foods, too. If I'm hankering for something unhealthy, then I love drinking a smoothie to help me fight it. My rule is that I drink a smoothie first, then, I see how severe my craving is. The great news is that the craving always goes away!

Smoothies are perfect if you're a busy person or if you're someone wanting a more energetic lifestyle or both! They're super easy to make, convenient for travel, delicious, and extraordinarily nutritious. They pack quite the punch! You get so much whole food nutrition packed in a smoothie, making them the perfect answer for helping people stay energized and focused all day long.

They take five minutes or less to make. And, making them right before you drink it is always the freshest way. However, if you're really tight on time, here is a helpful tip: Pick 3 days a week to make your smoothies, and then make enough to last for two days at a time. This is one of the things that can make them so easy and convenient. You can make a bunch in advance and store them in airtight containers in your refrigerator (I prefer glass mason jars... available and inexpensive at your local hardware store).

SMOOTHIE THINGS TO KNOW

When making your smoothie, consider the texture you're going after. Some people, like me, prefer nice thick smoothies that I can drink through my big glass straw. Some people, like my mom, prefer thinner smoothies, so she adds more water to her smoothies. And, some people prefer to actually eat their smoothies with a spoon; therefore, they use less water. When you're making the smoothies in the following recipes, keep in mind that the amount of water is just a suggestion. If you like your smoothie thin or thick, adjust the amount of water as necessary.

Some people prefer very cold and "shake-like" smoothies. If this is the case, then ice can be used or frozen fruit. A great and delicious tip is to always have frozen bananas on hand. The next time your bananas are at their "ripe" stage (with freckles), simply peel them and freeze in a Ziploc bag (or better yet, use a Food Saver™ like I do). I always have frozen bananas stored in my freezer ready to go for delicious and creamy smoothies.

You'll see that some of my recipes in this book call for the use of a green powder. This is to get an extra serving of concentrated greens into the day. My favorite brand is Vitamineral Green (you can find a link for it at KristensRaw.com/store). It's a great way to make your beverage extra alkaline and a nutritional powerhouse.

LET'S TALK ABOUT BLENDERS

Rest assured, you can make any of the smoothies, elixirs, and nut milks in this book with pretty much any ol' blender. However, if you want to really kick it up a notch, then a great addition to your kitchen is a powerful, high-speed blender. This appliance was game changing for me. A high-speed blender helps you get the most nutrition from your produce, because they have the ability to bust through the cell walls of the produce, releasing the nutrients (making them more accessible *and* easier to assimilate). Let's take lycopene for example. We've all heard that lycopene is most easily obtained from cooked tomatoes. Yes, it's good news that lycopene is released from cooked tomatoes. The bad news is that you destroy so many other nutrients from the cooking process. Well, people with high-speed blenders now have another option for getting lycopene from tomatoes, because high-speed blenders are so powerful that they break the cell walls of the uncooked tomatoes and release the lycopene. And... what about those pesky raspberry and strawberry seeds? High-speed blenders are reputed for crushing those, too.

Fresh smoothies and juices aren't the only reasons to get a high-speed blender though. They are great for making plenty of delicious and highly nutritious Raw vegan foods for you and your family, such as pate, pesto, soup, ice cream, mousse, nut/seed butter, and much more.

I'm always asked which high-speed blender is the best to get: Blendtec or Vita-Mix? Honestly, they're both terrific blenders and you'll likely be happy with whichever one you choose.

Here are some things to consider – keeping in mind that they're both fabulous and they'll both get the blending job done – a nice feature about the Blendtec is that it stores more easily on your counter top (under the cupboard due to it's size). However, a couple of great aspects about the Vita-Mix 5200 model is that it comes with a BPA-Free container and the Vita-Mix has a *much* better warranty than the Blendtec (as of the writing of this book). The Vita-Mix 5200 Model has a fantastic 7-year warranty (this warranty guarantees trouble-free performance under normal household use), while the Blendtec has a measly 3-year warranty on the base with only a 1-year warranty on the container.

So, they're both great machines and I have one of each. If I was hard pressed to pick one, I used to always say that I would pick the Blendtec. However, my heart has been won over by the Vita-Mix 5200 as of writing this book. I'm stoked about the BPA-Free container, their warranty, and the fantastic customer service they provide. Details for both machines are available at KristensRaw.com/store.

FRESH VEGGIE LIFE

Yield 1 serving

Here is a great recipe to make that is fresh and easy. It's especially terrific if you have some "leftover" veggies that you're eager to use up before your next shopping trip. Simply throw them in the blender with a few other ingredients. One of the best and fastest ways to get your veggies!

1 1/2 cups water
2 cups of any chopped veggies
1 tablespoon fresh herb(s), optional
fresh juice of 1 lemon
pinch salt
pinch black pepper

Blend all of the ingredients until smooth. You now have pure nutrition in a cup!

Variation:

- For a wonderfully decadent, satiating, and creamy Fresh Veggie Life, add 1/2 - 1 avocado (pitted and peeled) to your smoothie before blending.

LIQUID SALSA DANCE

Yield 1 serving

This recipe is fun and unique. If you're a fan of salsa, like me, then you'll love it. Tomatoes are a lovely source of vitamin C, potassium, as well as antioxidants.

    1 cup water
    2 tomatoes, chopped
    1/2 cucumber, peeled and chopped
    1/4 bunch cilantro, packed
    1 orange, peeled and seeded
    2 tablespoons fresh lime juice
    1/8 teaspoon cayenne, or to taste

Blend all of the ingredients in a blender until smooth, adding more water to get your desired consistency. You can drink this as a thick smoothie for a "filling" beverage or strain it through a nut milk bag and drink it as juice.

DAZZLING DAYLIGHT FLOWER SMOOTHIE

See photo at KristensRaw.com/photos.

Yield 3 cups

    2 large white peaches, pitted
    Juice of 1 lemon
    1 cup organic edible flowers

Blend the peaches and lemon juice until smooth. Add the flowers and pulse briefly. You want to have gorgeous flecks of colors showing. Enjoy served in a sassy wine glass or goblet.

RAW ARMOR

Yield 1 serving

I call this Raw Armor because it's filled with immune strengthening nutrients to help protect you and your health... just like armor would do.

Kale totally rocks the nutrition house! It's one of the most nutrient dense foods (we're talking vitamins A & C, potassium, iron, calcium, folate, and more!), and it's known for helping you fight and/or prevent cancer, promote eyesight, and more.

1 - 2 cups water, more if desired

2 large leaves kale

1 stalk celery, chopped

2 medium carrots, chopped

2 apples, cored and chopped

2 tablespoons fresh lemon juice

Blend all of the ingredients in a blender until smooth, adding more water to get your desired consistency. Drink it down and rule the world.

MOROCCAN BEACH SUNSET

Yield 1 serving

Here are some gorgeous Moroccan flavors that are sure to please you. I love carrots because they're filled with nutrition (beta-carotene, vitamins C & B-6, manganese, niacin, and potassium), *and* they're easy on the wallet. (Carrot side note: I love munching on fresh carrots when I go to the movie theater. Seriously, they're lightly sweet with a hefty crunch – perfect yum!)

1/2 cup water

1 cup carrot juice

1/2 cucumber, peeled and chopped

2 tablespoons raisins

1 orange, peeled and seeded

pinch cumin

pinch cinnamon

pinch nutmeg

Blend all of the ingredients in a blender until smooth, adding more water to get your desired consistency.

BEAUTY AND THE BEAST

Yield 1 serving

This reminds me of beauty and the beast, because the beauty of the smoothie is in all of the nutrition, but the beast of the smoothie is in the color.

Fresh mango is filled with vitamins C, A, K, and D, as well as calcium, magnesium, phosphorus, fiber, and more!

1/2 - 1 cup water

1/2 head romaine lettuce, chopped or 2 big handfuls of spinach

1/4 bunch parsley

1 large apple, chopped (you can leave the core in)

1 mango, peeled, pitted and chopped

1 tablespoon fresh mint

1 tablespoon fresh lime juice

Blend all of the ingredients in a blender until smooth, adding more water to get your desired consistency.

ENERGIZED WORKOUT SMOOTHIE

Yield 1 serving

This is one of the best smoothies to drink before, during and after your workout. The best thing to do is make a batch and drink most of it "before" your workout, reserving about 1/2 cup with which to water down and drink "during" your workout. Then, after your workout, make another one fresh right when you get home.

Celery's phtyonutrients have been shown to be one of the best ways to help attain healthy blood pressure, as well as helping build healthy bones.

1 cup water

2 bananas, peeled and chopped

1 - 2 stalks celery

pinch cinnamon

Blend all of the ingredients in a blender until smooth, adding more water to get your desired consistency.

KOWABUNGA MANGO KALE

Yield 1 serving

I love making smoothies with fresh organic mango, because it gives such a creamy texture. This smoothie is packed with nutrition and so easy to make. The perfect way to get your morning started.

> 1 cup of water, or more if desired
>
> 3 - 4 leaves of kale (I like lacinato kale the best, but any variety will work)
>
> 1 large mango, peeled, pitted and chopped

Combine everything in your blender and love it as you drink it. ☺

STRAWBERRY BANANA JUMP-START

See photo on cover and at KristensRaw.com/photos.

Yield 1 serving

The perfect way to start your day out right! Strawberries offer you vitamin C, folate, fiber, potassium, and powerful antioxidants (cancer- and heart disease-fighters).

> 1/2 - 1 cup water
>
> 2 bananas, peeled and chopped
>
> 1 pound strawberries, greens cut off

38

Blend all of the ingredients in a blender until smooth... or stop sooner if you like yours chunky!

LUSCIOUS PEAR

Yield 1 serving

Pears are lovely because they have a light and sweet flavor to them. They also contain potassium and vitamin C, as well as fiber and antioxidants. Their fiber is made up of soluble pectin (this helps keep you feeling full and it's shown to help reduce cholesterol).

1 cup water
2 pears, cored and chopped
2 soft dates, pitted
1/4 head of fennel, chopped
1/4 teaspoon vanilla extract
1/2 cup ice, optional

Blend all of the ingredients in a blender until smooth, adding more water to get your desired consistency.

SMOOTH AMBROSIA

Yield 1 serving

This is one of my favorites. It's so delicious and nutritious. The grapes, apple and orange are loaded with phytonutrients, and the coconut fills your body with wonderful electrolytes. A great combination.

1 cup green grapes

1 Granny Smith apple, cored and chopped

1 young Thai coconut water and meat

1 orange, peeled and seeded

Blend all of the ingredients in a blender until smooth, adding water to get your desired consistency.

OLD FAITHFUL

See photo on cover and at KristensRaw.com/photos.

Yield 1 serving

Nicely flavored. Inexpensive. Smooth and creamy. Definitely easy. What more could you ask for?

1 - 2 cups water

1 handful of any greens such as romaine or spinach

2 bananas, peeled and chopped

Blend the ingredients (adding more water, if necessary, to reach your desired consistency), and drink.

KRISTEN SUZANNE'S FAMOUS GREEN SMOOTHIE

Yield 1 serving

This smoothie is totally yummy, light, refreshing, and CHOCK-FULL of nutrition. Let's take a moment to concentrate on just the raspberries. They are a high fiber powerhouse. But, that's not all they bring to the table (or the smoothie, I should say). They have calcium, phosphorus, magnesium, potassium, and vitamins K & C.

    2 cups water

    1 cup raspberries

    1 Golden Delicious apple, chopped (including the core)

    1/2 cup cilantro, chopped

    1 stalk celery, chopped

    3 - 4 leaves of fresh basil

Blend all the ingredients until smooth. Enjoy.

VANILLA KIWI

Yield 1 serving

Simply delicious. I love drinking this as a night time snack. Kiwi is a powerhouse of nutrition. It's filled with an army of disease fighting phytonutrients, loads of vitamin C (twice as much as oranges!), magnesium, fiber & potassium.

    1 cup of water

    1 handful spinach

    3 kiwis, peeled and chopped

    1 banana, peeled and chopped

    1/2 teaspoon vanilla extract (or 1/2 vanilla bean, chopped)

Give everything a whirl in your blender and enjoy.

Z-TRAIN

Yield 1 serving

Okay... I had to name something after my dog, so this is it. (Z-Train is just one of many nicknames I have for him.) He brings me so much joy.

I love bananas in my smoothies because they give it such a lusciously creamy texture, not to mention a decadently sweet flavor. Oh, and how about a hat trick here... they're cheap!

2 cups water
2 bananas, peeled and chopped
2 soft dates, pitted
2 teaspoons raw carob powder
2 pinches cinnamon

Blend all of the ingredients in a blender until smooth, adding more water to get your desired consistency.

ZENERGIZING SMOOTHIE

Yield 1 serving

The green tea in this recipe creates a very Zen experience for you while drinking it. Green tea has been known to improve people's mood because of a substance found in it called "theanine." That's just one of many benefits green tea offers you. Be sure to buy organic green tea.*

1 cup green tea*

1 handful spinach

1 apple, cored and chopped

1 banana, peeled and chopped

pinch nutmeg

Blend all of the ingredients until smooth in a blender and enjoy your *Zen* state of mind!

* To prepare tea without using much heat, if any at all, place a mason jar with a cup of water on your counter. Place your organic green tea in it for 6 hours or more. Or, for a quicker version, warm the water on your stove and then steep the tea for no longer than three minutes.

DETOXIFYING SMOOTHIE

Yield 4 - 5 cups

Cilantro is known to help draw metals out of your body, so this smoothie is great for helping you detox. The ginger is beneficial for aiding circulation and digestion, and it is a rich source of antioxidants.

2 - 3 cups water

1/2 fresh pineapple, peeled, cored and chopped (or more)

1/2 bunch fresh cilantro (or more)

1/4 inch fresh ginger, peeled (or more)

Blend everything in your blender and enjoy this refreshing and detoxifying smoothie.

DRAGON BLOOD

Yield 1 - 2 servings

Let me tell you... this is *DELICIOUS!* And, it's extra nutritious. I could write paragraph after paragraph listing all the powerful nutrients in this smoothie, but this is a recipe book after all. Just trust me... Dragon Blood will make your body sing!

1 cup water
1/2 cup raspberries
1/2 cup strawberries, green stems removed
1/2 cup blackberries
1 apple, cored and chopped
1 orange, peeled and seeded
1/2 beet, chopped
1/4 inch ginger, peeled and chopped
1 tablespoon lime juice

Blend all of the ingredients in a blender until smooth, adding more water to get your desired consistency.

SPICY SUNRISE SMOOTHIE

See photo at KristensRaw.com/photos.

Yield approximately 5 cups

1 - 2 cups water (depending on how thick you like it)

(continued)

3 bananas, peeled and chopped

1 stalk celery, chopped

1 large carrot, chopped

1 red jalapeno pepper, stem and seeds removed

4 fresh mint leaves

Blend all of the ingredients until smooth. Enjoy!

SWEET LOW-SUGAR GREEN SMOOTHIE

Yield 1 serving

For a delicious green smoothie that is low in calories, but still nice and sweet, you have to try this!

2 cups water

1 - 2 handfuls of greens (I like parsley and spinach)

1/2 - 1 packet powdered stevia or 2 - 4 drops liquid stevia (or more to taste)

juice from 1 lime

Blend all of the ingredients in a blender and enjoy!

UN-FUZZY NAVEL

Yield 1 serving

This is a fun smoothie because of the party-time flavor. Here is an example of how adding a flavor extract to a smoothie can really kick it up a notch. When you think about it... smoothie recipes are endless. There are so many different combinations that you can make, it's impossible to ever get bored. Different fruits, different veggies, different extracts, different superfoods, etc... so many different combinations.

    1 - 2 cups water
    1 orange, peeled and seeded
    2 peaches, pitted
    1 - 2 soft dates, pitted
    1/4 teaspoon rum extract, more to taste

Blend all of the ingredients in a blender until smooth, adding more water to get your desired consistency.

PERFECT PEAR BANANA BLISS

Yield 1 serving

I'm in love with fruit smoothies and this one is fabulous. It's a terrific dessert, too! Next time you have a sweet tooth, make one of these. ☺

    2 cups water
    2 bananas, peeled and chopped
    1 pear, cored and chopped
    1/2 cup ice

Blend all of the ingredients in a blender until smooth, adding more water to get your desired consistency.

SWEET TART HERB

Yield 1 serving

This is a delightful smoothie that reminds me of sweet tarts. To change it up a bit, I like to add fresh herbs in my smoothies sometimes. They are packed full of nutrition and add so much flavor. I feel healthier with every sip.

1 1/2 cups water

2 - 3 Honey Crisp apples, cored and chopped

1 tablespoon fresh dill (or more)

1 tablespoon fresh lemon or lime juice

1 teaspoon fresh rosemary (or more)

Put the ingredients in a blender and blend away. Enjoy!

PINEAPPLE MANGO COLADA

Yield 2 - 4 servings (depends on how large you like your smoothie!)

Pineapple contains bromelain, which is a very rich source of enzymes known to greatly assist with digestion, wound healing, bruises, and reducing inflammation.

1/2 pineapple, peeled, cored and chopped

1 mango, peeled, pitted, and chopped (or 1 heaping cup frozen mango)

1 young Thai coconut, meat and water

(continued)

1/2 teaspoon rum extract (more to taste!)

2 tablespoons raw agave nectar

1 tablespoon fresh lime juice

1 cup ice cubes

Blend all of the ingredients together, except the ice. Add the ice and blend until desired texture is achieved.

BLUEBERRY POWER PACKER

Yield 1 quart

This smoothie is *packed* with nutrition, chlorophyll, and flavor.

For those of you who are new to hemp foods, hemp is basically one word: AMAZING. Hemp is commonly referred to as a "superfood" (okay, that makes it two words – haha – "amazing" and "superfood") because of its phenomenal nutritional value. Its amino acid profile dominates with the 8 essential amino acids (10 if you're elderly or a baby), making it a vegetarian source of "complete" protein!

Manitoba Harvest is my absolute favorite source for hemp products. For more recipes and information about hemp, be sure to check out my book, *Kristen Suzanne's Ultimate Raw Vegan Hemp Recipes.*

2 cups water

2 cups blueberries

1/4 cup hemp protein powder

1 tablespoon green powder

(continued)

1 tablespoon chia seeds

2 - 3 handfuls spinach

2 tablespoons fresh lemon juice

Blend this power packin' goodness up and enjoy some mega energy and fulfillment!

SPUMONI DESSERT SMOOTHIE

Yield 1 quart

I have been craving spumoni ice cream lately, so I had to come up with an alternative... *Raw Vegan style*. Here it is! Super delicious and yummy. Enjoy!

1 1/2 cups water

1 cup raw shelled pistachios, soaked 1 hour, drained and rinsed

1 (10oz) bag frozen cherries

1/4 cup raw agave nectar

3 tablespoons raw chocolate powder

1/2 teaspoon cherry extract

pinch Himalayan crystal salt

Blend until smooth and creamy. Enjoy!

LOVE NEST MACA SMOOTHIE

Yield 1 quart

Maca is known for having some amazing properties, which is why I was determined to make a recipe with this magical superfood. Personally, I usually can't stand the taste of it, but in this smoothie, I'm gung-ho for it.

The following are a few things maca is reputed for: balancing hormones, increasing strength and endurance, boosting libido, and fighting fatigue. It's a nutrient dense food. For details on where you can purchase maca, visit KristensRaw.com/store.

2 cups water

2 cups frozen raspberries

3 soft dates, pitted

1 tablespoon green powder

1 tablespoon raw carob powder

1 tablespoon chia seeds

2 - 3 teaspoons maca powder

3/4 teaspoon cherry extract

3/4 teaspoon cinnamon

Blend it up and enjoy!

CINNAMON KIWI GREEN SMOOTHIE

Yield 3 cups

Kiwi is a powerhouse of nutrition. It's filled with an army of disease fighting phytonutrients, loads of vitamin C (twice as much as oranges!), magnesium, fiber & potassium.

1 - 2 cups water (depending on the thickness desired)

1 large handful spinach

1 kiwi (peeled or not, it's up to you; I peel 1/2 of mine and leave the peel on the other half)

1 whole apple, chopped (yep, core and all)

3/4 teaspoon cinnamon

Blend this sassy smoothie up and enjoy the powers of vitamins, minerals, and phytonutrients going to work for you. YUMMY!

ISLAND OASIS GIRL

Yield 3 cups

This smoothie is heavenly and takes my mind far away from every day activities with every sip. It's a vacation in a cup! You just might want to put on your sunglasses while enjoying this (even if you're indoors – *who cares?!?!*)

1/2 cup water

1 cup fresh orange juice

1 (10oz) bag frozen mango (or 2 cups fresh mango, peeled and pitted)*

1 small banana, peeled

1 teaspoon rum extract

1 teaspoon coconut extract**

Blend all of the ingredients together until smooth. Sit back, relax and enjoy every sip.

* I prefer frozen mango because it makes the drink refreshing, thick, and cold, which is perfect on a hot day.

** Available at www.frontiercoop.com

SWEET DESSERT SMOOTHIE

Yield approximately 4 cups

Smoothies should NOT be just for breakfast. Some of the best smoothies are made wonderfully sweet and the perfect finale to a delicious meal. This is one heck of a healthy dessert!!!

    2 cups water
    2 bananas, peeled
    6 - 7 soft dates, pitted (I use 7 ☺)
    1/4 cup Artisana Raw Vegan Amazon Bliss*
    3/4 teaspoon hazelnut extract
    3/4 teaspoon coffee extract
    1/4 teaspoon cinnamon
    1 cup ice

Blend all of the ingredients together, except the ice. Add the ice and blend. Serve in chilled glass mugs and enjoy!

* This is available in most Whole Foods Markets or online.

BLUEBERRY CARDAMOM BREAKFAST SMOOTHIE

Yield 1 large serving

Blueberries are total brain food and rank among the highest for antioxidants. They are full of nutrition. I love blueberries.

Cardamom, member of the ginger family, is an ancient spice, which is known for stimulating bile flow for a healthy liver and metabolism of fat. It contains essential oils with high antioxidant properties.

2 cups water

2 cups frozen organic blueberries

2 frozen organic bananas

1/4 teaspoon cardamom (ground)

1/8 teaspoon cinnamon

Give everything a whirl in your blender and enjoy this fabulous breakfast of real champions.

DANCING GREEN SMOOTHIE

Yield 1 quart

When I drink this, it makes me want to get up an dance. Can't help myself. It has so much super power nutrition with all of the antioxidants, essential fatty acids, and essential amino acids. ☺

2 cups water

2 bananas, peeled

1/2 bunch cilantro

2 tablespoons hemp protein powder

(continued)

1 tablespoon chia seeds

2 tablespoon goji berries

1 teaspoon raw carob or raw chocolate powder

1 teaspoon green powder

1/4 teaspoon cinnamon

smidge cayenne pepper (or more!!!)

Give it a whirl in your blender, drink it down, and dance your heart out!

CRANBERRY DELIGHT

Yield approximately 1 quart

There are plenty of reasons to add cranberries to your diet, but most people only think about cranberries around the holidays. These little red pearls of tartness present you with vitamin C, dietary fiber, vitamin K, manganese, and more. We, women, know they're wonderful for helping prevent and treat urinary tract infections, too.

1 1/2 cups water

3 bananas, peeled

3/4 cup fresh cranberries* (depending the level of tartness desired)

Blend all of the ingredients until smooth and enjoy.

* If you don't have fresh cranberries available to you at the time, then you can substitute with frozen cranberries. One thing I like to do is buy loads of fresh cranberries when they are in season during the fall. Then, I freeze them in glass

mason jars (or bags with my Food Saver™) until I'm ready to use them.

FRAGRANT PEACH GREEN SMOOTHIE

Yield approximately 5 cups

Peaches are among my favorites when it comes to fruit. I love how juicy they get, making them perfect for smoothies. Peaches contain fiber, calcium, magnesium, vitamin C, phosphorus, potassium, and more.

    2 cups water
    2 large white peaches, pitted
    1 banana, peeled
    1 large handful spinach
    1 small handful fresh basil
    1 tablespoon fresh rosemary

Blend all of the ingredients together until smooth and creamy (making sure the rosemary and basil get blended in nicely).

FLUFFY GREEN SMOOTHIE

Yield 1 serving

This is one of my favorite fall season smoothies. It's full of nutrition and easy on the wallet.

I love how the apples make this "fluffy" and the spinach adds a nice creaminess to it.

1 1/2 - 2 cups water

2 apples, cored and chopped

2 handfuls spinach

1/2 teaspoon cinnamon

Blend the ingredients until smooth.

FLUFFY GREEN PROTEIN SMOOTHIE

Yield 1 serving

This recipe is similar to the one above but with protein and green powder. Yowza!

1 1/2 - 2 cups water

2 apples, cored and chopped

2 handfuls spinach

2 tablespoons hemp protein powder

2 teaspoons green powder

1/2 teaspoon cinnamon

Blend the ingredients until smooth.

PURE DELIGHT GREEN SMOOTHIE

Yield 1 serving

Here is a great smoothie recipe that is perfect for summer. It's simple, delicious, delightful, refreshing, light, nourishing, beautiful, and vibrant. And, guess what? That's how you'll feel after only one sip (or gulp, in my case!).

1 cup water

2 medium bananas, peeled and chopped

2 medium lacinato kale leaves

1 cucumber, chopped

Give this energy filled lusciousness a whirl in your blender and enjoy with delight.

HAPPY BUNNY

Yield 2 1/2 cups

Super easy and gorgeously orange. This light smoothie will fill you with energy and nutrients from head to toe, including essential amino acids, vitamins, minerals, and fiber.

2 cups water

1 cup carrots, chopped

2 tablespoons goji berries

Blend the ingredients in your blender for 45 - 60 seconds. At this point you can pour it into your favorite glass and enjoy, or you can blend in a cup of ice to make it more "shake" like. I like it both ways!

CHAPTER 3

NUT/SEED MILKS & SHAKES

NATURE'S HEALTHY ALTERNATIVE TO MILK

Having a substitute for dairy is important in many households. Raw nut/seed milk is perfect for the job. These cow dairy substitutes are so creamy, sweet, delicious, and can be used in a number of ways. And, Raw nut/seed milks are dairy-free and preservative-free. The following recipes will stay fresh when stored in an airtight container (glass mason jars are perfect) for up to 5 days. They also freeze wonderfully! This is great because you can make a few large batches and freeze them in small to medium sized glass mason jars. Then, take one out of the freezer the night before you plan on drinking it, and let it begin thawing in the refrigerator.

These milks can be used in smoothies, soups, poured over cereal, desserts, or simply alongside a plate of delicious cookies. I think it's neat that my friend's son loves having a tall glass of cold hemp milk after school everyday. His mom is very proud!

THE 1-MINUTE NUT MILK

Yield 2 cups

This makes life easy. Knowing that you can whip up a super fast nut or seed milk in less than a minute! This is perfect for those of us with busy lifestyles, people who are on the run, or for those of us who simply forget to soak nuts/seeds overnight as usually needed in traditional recipes.

It's a good idea to double the recipe and have it ready to enjoy all week.

2 cups water

2 - 3 tablespoons raw nut or seed butter

1 - 2 soft dates, pitted or 1 tablespoon raw agave nectar, optional

Blend all of the ingredients together until smooth and creamy.

1-MINUTE CHOCOLATE NUT MILK

Yield 2 cups

For those of us on the run, or if you forgot to soak your nuts overnight, here is another quick 1-minute nut milk you can enjoy, but this one is for chocolate lovers.

2 cups water

2 - 3 tablespoons raw nut or seed butter

1 - 2 soft dates, pitted or 1 tablespoon raw agave nectar, optional

1 - 2 tablespoons raw chocolate powder or raw carob powder

Blend all of the ingredients together until smooth and creamy.

60

CREAMY DREAMY NUT/SEED MILK

Yield approximately 3 cups

> 1 1/2 cups nuts or seeds, soaked 6 - 8 hours, drained and rinsed*
> 3 1/4 cups water
> 2 soft dates, pitted (or 1 tablespoon raw agave nectar)
> pinch sea salt, optional

Blend all of the ingredients together until smooth and creamy. Enjoy!

* If you're using hemp seeds there is no need to soak them, but you may (or may not) choose to add more water depending on the texture you want.

Variation:

- Strain through a nut milk bag for an even smoother milk

CINNAMON PECAN MILK

Yield approximately 5 cups

This is perfect poured over Raw granola. I also love drinking this as a dessert or as a filling, mid-day snack. Cinnamon Pecan Milk is both dairy-free and preservative-free. Fresh nut or seed milks are the healthiest alternatives to cow's milk.

1 cup cashews, soaked 1 hour, drained and rinsed

1/2 cup pecans, soaked 4 - 6 hours, drained and rinsed

3 1/2 cups water (or more)

3 soft dates, pitted

2 tablespoons raw agave nectar

1 1/2 teaspoons cinnamon

1/2 teaspoon vanilla extract

Blend all of the ingredients until smooth, adding more water until you reach your desired consistency. For an extra smooth texture, strain the nut milk through a nut milk bag.

Variations:

- You can use any combination of nuts, but keep in mind that cashews keep it extra creamy
- Feel free to alter the sweetness, or omit the dates and agave

ROCKIN' MACA CHOCOLATE SHAKE

Yield 1 - 2 servings

This shake will truly rock your world! Be prepared for unstoppable energy and endurance after you drink this baby!

Raw cacao is reputed for being a super food because it's loaded with antioxidants (and I mean it... loaded!). It also has protein and fiber.

1 cup water, more if desired

(continued)

1 young Thai coconut, water and meat

2 tablespoons raw chocolate powder

2 tablespoons raw agave nectar

1 tablespoon raw cacao nibs

2 - 3 teaspoons raw maca powder

1/4 teaspoon cinnamon

pinch salt, optional

1/2 - 1 cup ice

Blend all of the ingredients together, except the ice, until smooth and creamy. Add the ice and blend briefly for a fabulous shake.

CARAMEL CHOCOLATE SHAKE

Yield 2 servings

This is a real treat of a shake. Super yummy! I oftentimes make this as a dessert shake.

Did you know that carob is a member of the pea family? It's a great source of protein and fiber. It also contains many minerals, vitamins, and antioxidants. Carob is especially helpful with digestive challenges.

3 cups *Raw Nut/Seed Milk* (see recipe p. 25)

4 soft dates, pitted

2 tablespoons raw chocolate powder

1 tablespoon raw carob powder

1 teaspoon mesquite meal powder*

(continued)

1 teaspoon lucuma powder*

1/4 teaspoon vanilla extract

pinch salt, optional

1 cup ice

Blend all of the ingredients, except the ice, until smooth and creamy. Add the ice and blend briefly for a decadent shake.

* Available from Navitas Naturals (online or at some Whole Foods Markets)

EARTHBOUND BRAZIL NUT MILK

See photo at KristensRaw.com/photos.

Yield 3 cups

This is one of my favorite nut milks because it has such a rich, earthy delicious flavor. It's SO good!

Brazil nuts are one of the best sources available for selenium, a very important trace element. They also contain protein, fiber, and calcium.

2 cups water (use the amount for the consistency you desire)

1 cup Brazil nuts, unsoaked

3 soft dates, pitted

1 1/2 teaspoons mesquite powder*

1/4 teaspoon cinnamon

pinch nutmeg

pinch sea salt

Blend all of the ingredients until rich, smooth and creamy. Enjoy this satiating nut milk any time of the day.

* Available from Navitas Naturals (online or at some Whole Foods Markets)

Variations:

- For an extra treat, add 1 - 2 teaspoons of Raw carob powder
- Want a little fun crunch? Add a small handful of cacao nibs

CARDAMOM MILK

Yield 2 cups

Cardamom, member of the ginger family, is an ancient spice, which is known for stimulating bile flow for a healthy liver and metabolism of fat. It contains essential oils with high antioxidant properties.

But, that's not all. Cardamom, with its calming effect on the digestive system, is also helpful if you have gas.

2 cups *Raw Nut/Seed Milk* (see recipe p. 25)

2 - 3 teaspoons raw agave nectar or 1 - 2 soft dates, pitted (if the Raw Nut/Seed Milk you use is unsweetened)

1/2 teaspoon cardamom seeds

Grind the cardamom seeds in a coffee grinder or a mortar and pestle. Transfer the ground seeds to a blender and add the remaining ingredients and blend. Enjoy!

MY MOCHA LATTE FIX

Yield 2 servings

For those of us still wanting a triple venti soy latte from our friendly coffeehouse, this is a helpful substitute that is healthy and fun. To make it extra special, serve it in your favorite coffee mug(s)!

You can use whatever nuts you have on hand. I like Brazil nuts for their earthy flavor and I like cashews for the creamy texture they offer.

2 cups water, or more, depending on how thick you want it

3/4 cup Brazil nuts, unsoaked

1/2 cup cashews, soaked 1 hour, rinsed and drained

2 soft dates, pitted

1 tablespoon raw chocolate powder

2 teaspoons raw agave nectar

3/4 teaspoon coffee extract

1/4 teaspoon cinnamon

1/2 vanilla bean, optional, but worth it!

pinch nutmeg

pinch cayenne pepper (or more to really give it some "heat")

pinch sea salt, optional

Blend all of the ingredients until rich, smooth and creamy. Enjoy this satiating nut milk any time of the day.

FENNEL SEED MILK

Yield 2 cups

This is a delicious and fun alternative to the normal nut and seed milk recipes.

2 cups *Raw Nut/Seed Milk* (see recipe p. 25)
2 - 3 teaspoons raw agave nectar or 1 - 2 soft dates, pitted (if the Raw Nut/Seed Milk you use is unsweetened)
1/2 teaspoon fennel seeds

Blend all of the ingredients in a blender until smooth and creamy. Enjoy!

CARROT SPICED MILKSHAKE

Yield 2 cups

This is such a fun alternative to regular nut milk. Pour this on your next bowl of cereal for some vibrant fun. Or, enjoy it as a satiating afternoon snack. I've even enjoyed it as a dessert! The recipe calls for any type of Raw nut/seed milk, but one of my favorite versions is with Raw Pecan Nut Milk. Yum!

1 1/2 cups *Raw Nut/Seed Milk* (see recipe p. 25)
2 medium carrots, chopped
dash nutmeg
dash cinnamon
1 clove

Blend all of the ingredients thoroughly (approximately 45 - 60 seconds). Enjoy!

WARM PISTACHIO MILK

Yield 1 1/2 cups

If you like pistachios, then you'll love this recipe. It's wonderfully creamy.

1 cup water

1 cup pistachios, shelled, soaked 4 - 6 hours, drained and rinsed

1 tablespoon lucuma powder*

1 teaspoon raw agave nectar or 1 soft date, pitted

Blend all of the ingredients thoroughly (approximately 1 minute). Enjoy!

* Available at NavitasNaturals.com

CHAPTER 4

PLANT BLOOD

THE STUFF OF LIFE!

I call any freshly juiced fruits or vegetables "Plant Blood" because... that's what it *IS*. (Not to mention, it sounds very cool!) Like the vegan version of being a vampire, I feel absolutely super-human when I'm drinking it down. Plant Blood is packed with vitamins, minerals and phytonutrients. Fruit in juices are known to be cleansing, while vegetables and greens are recognized as rebuilding and regenerating.

Fresh fruit and vegetable juices can do wonders for your body, spirit and mind. They can help you cleanse your body. They can fill you up with energy because you're giving your digestion a rest with the removal of the fiber. They can make the cells in your body happy because you're giving them vital nutrients. Everyone should be drinking fresh Plant Blood from toddler to senior, whether you're 100% Raw or 10% Raw.

TIPS & TRICKS FOR MAKING THE BEST PLANT BLOOD EVER

Here are a variety of tips and tricks that you might find useful when making and drinking Plant Blood:

- For people struggling with caffeine, it can help to add carrot juice to some of your morning juices
- Add beets once in a while for extra nutrition (don't be alarmed if you pee red shortly after drinking!)

- Add a clove of garlic for immune strengthening benefits
- Add 1/4 inch of fresh ginger for digestive and circulation enhancing properties
- If you see lemons or limes called for in the following recipes then you can do any of the following:
  - Squeeze in the juice from the citrus *after* using your juicer
  - Peel the citrus and then juice the flesh like you do your other ingredients
  - Juice the whole citrus (peel and flesh) if your juicer can handle it (refer to your juicer's manual for instructions)
- If you find that you've made a juice that is too "green" for your taste try adding any of the following:
  - Water: simply water it down by dividing it between two glass mason jars and filling them up with extra water
  - Fresh lemon or lime juice
  - Stevia (liquid, powder, or fresh leaves)
  - Pinch or two of Himalayan crystal salt
  - Another cucumber and/or some celery juiced into it
  - Garlic, ginger, cayenne, cinnamon, turmeric, nutmeg, etc
  - Organic extracts (vanilla, lemon, orange, maple, cherry, coconut, etc).

MY FAVORITE JUICERS

Which juicer is my favorite? The answer is that I actually have two, and I love them both for different reasons. The two juicers I use:

Green Star

This bad boy isn't cheap, but it's life changing. This machine is great because it's extremely durable, reliable, juices wheatgrass (most juicers cannot do this, so you often have to buy a separate wheatgrass juicer), plus more. Because this juicer uses twin gears, which gently and slowly extract the juice, it doesn't degrade or oxidize nearly as fast as it does with a centrifugal juicer (details about centrifugal juicer below). Green Star juice can be stored in an airtight container for a couple of days, when stored properly, without much oxidation, which makes it perfect for people who can only juice once a day or less.

This juicer squeezes out every bit of juice, leaving you with very dry pulp, so you're really getting your money's worth from your organic produce. Here are other things the Green Star Juicer can do: make ice cream from frozen produce such as bananas or mangoes, as well as homogenize nuts, seeds and grains for pate and butters, and more.

The Green Star takes longer to use and clean up, but it's still amazing and well worth the money (and the time if you have it). I have a Green Star and don't use it as much as I used to now that I have the Breville (details below), but there are times I still rely on it. That's for sure!

Breville Fountain Juicer

This juicer has a special place in my heart. I LOVE my Breville Fountain Juicer (and pretty much use it daily) because it's lightening fast and SUPER EASY to clean. This machine inspires me to juice multiple times a day due to its ease of use. It's considerably less expensive than the Green Star, but because it's centrifugal, you should drink the juice within 15 minutes of making it to prevent oxidation and nutrient loss.

This is the perfect juicer for people who plan to do a lot of daily juicing, and want it to be fast and efficient — just be sure to *drink right after juicing*. The other thing to note is that the pulp from this juicer is quite moist, so you know that you're not extracting all of the juice like you do with the Green Star. However, I usually add the pulp to my dog's food or put it on top of my salad or feed it to the bunnies in my yard or make raw dehydrated crackers from it (so, you can see, it doesn't go to waste).

All in all, I love both of my juicers and I'm happy to have and use both. I find that I drink a lot more juice having the Breville due to its ease of use and cleaning, but I love having my Green Star for times I juice wheatgrass, make other things besides juice, or for those days that I need to make my juice ahead of time.

Just Because You Don't Have a Juicer Doesn't Mean You Can't Juice!

That's right! You can juice without a juicer. What you will need is... your blender and a nut milk bag (or a paint straining bag from the hardware store – much less expensive).

Basically what you do is follow one the recipes below, but add a cup of water (more if necessary) to the recipe. Blend it all up with your blender until it's like a smoothie. Then, strain the juice, using a nut milk bag to keep the pulp separate, into a large bowl. Transfer the fresh juice to a glass mason jar (or your choice of a drinking glass) and voila! Fresh Plant Blood – made without a juicer. I recommend consuming this juice right after making it, like with the Breville model, to prevent further oxidation.

THE ORIGINAL PLANT BLOOD

Yield 1 - 2 servings

This juice covers all the bases when it comes to loading you up with phenomenal nutrition. This is so good!

5 leaves kale
5 stalks celery
1/2 bunch parsley
2 - 3 carrots
1 apple
1 lemon
1 cucumber
1/4 inch piece of ginger

Juice all of the ingredients.

GREEN MACHINE

See photo at KristensRaw.com/photos.

Yield 1 - 2 servings

This juice is fantastic. It loads you with nutrients and energy, and it's super duper delicious.

1 large cucumber
1/2 bunch celery
1/2 bunch parsley
1 green apple

Juice all of the ingredients and enjoy!

VITALITY JUICE

Yield 1 - 2 servings

Dandelion, a natural diuretic, is excellent for cleansing the liver. It's bitter, however, so it's best juiced with something sweet.

- 4 stalks celery
- 1 cucumber
- 1 zucchini
- 5 leaves dinosaur kale
- 1 pear or apple
- 4 leaves dandelion

Juice all of the ingredients.

REFRESHING MORNING

Yield 1 - 2 servings

Nice, light, refreshing, cooling... perfect for your morning.

- 1 large cucumber
- 1 zucchini
- 1 apple
- 3 - 4 leaves kale

Juice all of the ingredients and enjoy!

ANTIOXIDANT POWERHOUSE

Yield 1 - 2 servings

Broccoli is one of the best foods you can consume to help prevent and/or fight cancer. Broccoli on its own, I'm not a huge fan of the flavor... but broccoli with carrots (or apples)? Sign me up!

5 carrots
1 head broccoli, including stalk

Juice all of the ingredients.

LIGHT-N-LIVELY

Yield 1 - 2 servings

Parsley is purifying, detoxifying, and deodorizing because it's loaded with chlorophyll. This anticancer green is also filled with nutrients for eye and bone health.

2 lemons
1/2 bunch celery
2 cucumbers
1 bunch parsley

Juice all of the ingredients.

SPROUT POWER

Yield 1 - 2 servings

Sprouts ROCK! They are full of seriously intense nutrition that is very easy to digest and assimilate. Sprouts are one of the most concentrated sources of vitamins, minerals, enzymes, and amino acids. Sprouts are really inexpensive and fun to grow all by yourself. For details on how to grow your own sprouts, check out my blog post:

www.kristensraw.blogspot.com/2008/04/this-is-how-i-sprout-easy-directions.html

> 1 lemon or lime
> 1 orange, peeled
> 2 cucumbers
> 2 large handfuls sprouts
> 2 handfuls spinach
> 1/4 inch fresh ginger

Juice all of the ingredients.

BELLA'S ETERNAL LOVE

Yield 1 - 2 servings

I love bell peppers. When I'm not juicing them, you can often find me eating one just like an apple. They're low in calories and have vitamins A, K & C, potassium and lycopene.

> 3 - 4 red, orange or yellow bell peppers, destemmed
> 1/2 bunch celery
> 1 bunch parsley
> 1/4 cup fresh basil
> 1 tablespoon fresh oregano

Juice all of the ingredients.

SUPER DISCO GREEN JUICE

Yield 1 - 2 servings

This juice is named Super Disco Green Juice because with every sip, the cells in your body will think you're playing disco music for them, and they're going to want to get up and dance for you. The broccoli is hardcore for fighting and helping prevent cancer. The carrots, cucumber, ginger and citrus bring loads of nutrition to the table as well. Drink on... Dance on...

   1 head broccoli (including stalk)
   3 carrots
   1/2 lemon
   1 lime
   1 cucumber
   1/4 inch fresh ginger

Juice the ingredients and enjoy.

ITALLION STALLION

Yield 1 - 2 servings

I'm Italian and I love Italian flavors so I wanted a juice just like that. The garlic is delicious in it. This is a particularly good recipe when you're juice feasting because it doesn't remind you of a juice, so much, as it does food because of the flavors in it. It's very satiating in that way.

1 medium tomato

1 zucchini

1 cup spinach, packed

1 large cucumber

1/2 head fennel

4 leaves fresh basil

1 small clove garlic

Juice all of the ingredients.

SWEET TART JUICE

Yield 1 - 2 servings

This is amazing! It tastes like a sweet tart.

1 lemon

2 pears

2 tart apples

1 large cucumber

Juice all of the ingredients.

STRAIGHT UP CARROT CELERY COMBO

Yield 1 - 2 servings

This is so simple and delicious. You get sweetness from the carrots complimented with a nicely light, natural saltiness from the celery. This is really good.

5 - 7 carrots
1/2 bunch celery

Juice the carrots and celery and drink up.

CILANTRO ARUGULA COMBO

Yield 1 - 2 servings

Arugula is a low calorie green that provides you with folate, vitamins A & K, iron, and lutein. It gives this juice a lovely peppery flavor.

1/2 bunch cilantro
1/4 bunch arugula
4 stalks celery
2 carrots
1 large cucumber
1/4 teaspoon cinnamon
pinch nutmeg

Juice all of the ingredients, except the cinnamon and nutmeg. Just before drinking, stir in the cinnamon and nutmeg.

"TAKE THE EDGE OFF" CARROT-APPLE

Yield 1 - 2 servings

I call this juice "Take the Edge Off" because that's exactly what it does when you're craving anything sweet. If you're afraid you might lose control of your sweet tooth and eat something unhealthy, then this is one of the best things you can do to immediately fix it. Trust me, it works.

2 apples
5 carrots

Juice the apples and carrots and enjoy this sweet, refreshing, and completely satiating beverage.

PINEAPPLE CILANTRO TANGO

Yield 1 - 2 servings

This is so delicious! Cilantro has been shown to draw heavy metals out of the body, making this a very detoxifying juice. If you don't like cilantro, then replace it with parsley or spinach (not liking cilantro might be the result of having too much metal in your body and once you're more "cleaned out" you might enjoy it).

1/2 pineapple, peeled (including 1/2 of the core – lots of nutrition in the core!)
1/2 bunch of fresh cilantro
4 - 5 fresh mint leaves
1 large cucumber

Juice all of the ingredients and enjoy!

SEXY RED

Yield 1 - 2 servings

Beets are full of vitamins, which make this a very nourishing plant blood. Uhmm, watch out and don't be alarmed if you're eliminating anything from your body that is "red" in color after drinking this. It's probably from the beets.

1 beet

3/4 cup fresh cranberries

2 apples

1 pint strawberries, whole

pinch cayenne pepper

Juice all of the ingredients except the cayenne pepper. I like to leave on the strawberry stems to get some extra green in my diet, but you can take them off. Stir in the cayenne and drink right away.

KITCHEN SINK JUICES (AND SMOOTHIES)

This is so much fun! The premise here is knowing that any fresh produce you find Raw and "leftover" in your refrigerator can pretty much be used to make a wonderfully nutritious and fresh juice. You can do this in your blender or juicer. Basically, it can have everything in it, but the kitchen sink – ha ha.

If you're using a blender, start with 1 - 2 cups of water, depending on how many water rich veggies and fruits you have to use. And then start adding things... this could include garlic, herbs, zucchini, tomatoes, celery, beets, ginger, lime and lemon juice, banana, apple, any or all of these things. Blend or juice them up and taste. The thing to remember with smoothies and juices is that you can drink them down quickly. So, be hard-core about it. Whatever you make, just drink it down even if it doesn't taste the best, because you know you're getting the greatest nutrition possible. Odds are that it'll be delicious... but in case you put a little too much of something bitter and you don't have a little agave nectar on hand to correct it, just "plug-n-chug" (plug your nose and drink it down, baby!)

In addition to the suggestions above, to help ensure a delicious and refreshing juice or smoothie, consider adding any of the following: something with a sour note (lemon or lime juice) and maybe something sweet (carrot, apple, orange, or even a little Raw agave nectar). You can also add herbs for flavor, which give superior nutrition and/or maybe some fresh ginger or garlic. I love adding mint and ginger to my juice recipes.

Get creative and don't be scared. It's empowering! Start with the basics and taste as you go along... adding things until you're happy. And, most importantly... don't forget to write it down! Believe me, there's nothing worse than coming up with a fabulous recipe and not writing it down.

CHAPTER 5

ELIXIRS

ANCIENT SECRETS NEVER TASTED SO GOOD!

For centuries, "elixirs" were used as tinctures to heal people or bring about other desired effects such as boosting stamina or potency. While the following elixirs are not necessarily designed to "heal" you of anything (the FDA frowns upon such claims, despite our learning a thing or two through 2000 years of trial and error), they'll certainly make you feel great when you are drinking them.

So, prepare one of these wonderful elixirs, sit back, and feel fantastic. Here's to your health!

YOUTHFUL ELIXIR

Yield 1 - 2 servings

Berries have so many potent antioxidants in them, making them ideal for helping to fight aging and helping us stay young in heart, mind and body.

1/2 cup water

1 cup strawberries, green stems removed

1 cup blueberries

(continued)

1/2 cup raspberries

1 lemon, peeled and halved

1 cucumber, peeled and chopped

Blend all of the ingredients together in your blender. Strain through a nut milk bag. Drink it down and enjoy all of the nutrients going to work on fighting the aging process.

GRAPEFRUIT ELIXIR

Yield 1 serving

This is a very refreshing drink if you like grapefruits. Enjoy.

1 cup fresh grapefruit juice

1/2 cup berries of your choice

1 - 2 soft dates, pitted or 2 - 3 teaspoons raw agave nectar

1/2 - 1 cup water

Blend all of the ingredients in a blender until smooth, adding more water to get your desired consistency.

VACATION ELIXIR

Yield 2 servings

This is such a refreshing, tropical flavored experience. You'll think you've been transported to Mexico for a relaxing vacation as you sip this delicious elixir.

1/2 pineapple, peeled, cored and chopped

1 mango, peeled, pitted and chopped

water from 1 young Thai coconut*

1 tablespoon coconut oil

1/2 teaspoon rum extract

1 tablespoon raw agave nectar

2 tablespoons fresh squeezed lime juice

Blend all of the ingredients until smooth. Strain through a nut milk bag and enjoy.

* If you aren't using the meat of the coconut for anything, simply freeze it for a later use.

POWER ENERGY ELIXIR

Yield 1 serving

This elixir was born to help give you true, sustainable energy. *Warning:* it's not particularly tasty, but for those of us who are hard core... we don't care. Just mix it up and drink it down. Or, as I like to say... "Plug-n-Chug!"

1/2 cup water

Juice from 2 oranges

1 tablespoon green powder (or more!)

2 teaspoons maca powder (or more!)

1 teaspoon carob powder

1/4 teaspoon cinnamon

Place all of the ingredients in a glass mason jar and shake it up to thoroughly mix. Drink it down (this is just one of those concoctions that is best gulped instead of sipped). Feel the buzz of energy take you over and carry you through your day.

CITRUS ZING ELIXIR

See photo at KristensRaw.com/photos.

Yield 1 serving

This refreshing drink is perfect after a sweaty workout to replenish you with natural electrolytes and antioxidants. It's so delicious.

    1 cup young Thai coconut water
    1/4 cup water
    juice from 1 orange
    1/4 cup fresh lemon juice
    1 tablespoon fresh lime juice
    1/4 teaspoon fresh ginger, grated
    1 tablespoon goji berries
    2 soft dates, pitted or 1 tablespoon raw agave nectar

Blend all of the ingredients and drink!

Variation:

- For a thicker elixir, include the meat from the young Thai coconut

SWEET MINT RELAXER ELIXIR

Yield 1 serving

This is a nice beverage to drink when you're ready to relax and wind down for the evening. Ahhhhh, so nice.

1 - 2 drops peppermint oil or extract
2 drops liquid stevia or dash of powder (more to taste)
1 cup warm water

Put the peppermint oil (or extract) and stevia in your favorite mug. Add the warm water and enjoy.

SWEET MINT REFRESHER ELIXIR

Yield 1 serving

This is a nice refresher in the morning or before (and during) a sweaty workout!

1 - 2 drops peppermint oil or extract
2 drops liquid stevia or dash of powder (more to taste)
1 1/2 cups water
1 cup ice

Put the peppermint oil (or extract) and stevia in a glass. Add the water and stir. Add the ice. Enjoy!

LEMON MINT COOLER ELIXIR

Yield 1 serving

This is wonderful as an afternoon refresher to help "pick you up."

1 tablespoon fresh lemon or lime juice

1 - 2 drops peppermint oil or extract

2 drops liquid stevia or dash of powder (more to taste)

1 1/2 cups water

1 cup ice

1 tablespoon fresh mint leaves, optional

Put the fresh lemon or lime juice, peppermint oil (or extract), and stevia in a glass. Add the water and stir to mix. Add the ice. Optional, stir in the fresh mint or use as a garnish.

ROMANTIC CLOVE ELIXIR

Yield 1 serving

Cloves are potent, making them perfect for an elixir. They are considered an important spice for energy circulation in Asian medicine. Cloves are also reputed for fighting bacteria and viruses. Some of the nutrients you'll find in cloves include: calcium, phytosterols, potassium, manganese, as well as fiber.

1 cup warm water

2 cloves, crushed

1/2 teaspoon raw agave nectar or 2 drops liquid stevia

1 slice of orange

Stir the warm water, cloves, and agave together in your favorite mug and allow it to sit for 10 minutes. Strain out the cloves, garnish with orange, and enjoy.

WARMING THAI ELIXIR

Yield 1 serving

Thai flavors are among my favorite. The ginger juice in this recipe aids in circulation, which can help "warm" you.

1 cup young Thai coconut water
1 tablespoon fresh ginger juice*
1 teaspoon raw agave nectar or 2 drops of liquid stevia
pinch cinnamon

Place the ingredients in your favorite mug and stir. You may warm it in a dehydrator if you like.

* To make frozen ginger cubes to have on hand, juice fresh whole ginger. Then, freeze the fresh ginger juice in an ice cube tray for 24 hours. Remove the frozen ginger juice cubes from the ice cube tray and store them in a jar or a Ziploc baggie in your freezer. Simply take one out to thaw when a recipe calls for fresh ginger juice.

SOOTHING SWEET GINGER ELIXIR

Yield 1 serving

This is excellent for a cold night or if you have an upset stomach... or just anytime. It's very satiating and I like to drink a cup if I'm starting to crave anything unhealthy. It helps me fight off any cravings in the moment.

1 cup warm water

1 tablespoon fresh grated ginger or fresh ginger juice

1/2 - 1 packet of stevia (or 2 - 3 drops liquid stevia) or 1 teaspoon raw agave nectar

Stir the ingredients together and enjoy.

RAW FRUIT WATER ELIXIR

See photo at KristensRaw.com/photos.

This makes water fun, delicious and so beautiful – perfect for entertaining and impressing guests! The fruits add just a hint of flavor. Drink it from a glamorous wine glass for an even better effect.

pitcher of water

various pieces/slices of fruits – some of my favorites are berries, melons, cucumber, and citrus.

Place all of the ingredients in a water pitcher and allow it to sit in your refrigerator for a few hours. When you pour your Raw Fruit Water into a glass, allow some pieces of the fruit to go in to each glass.

Variations:

- Add 1/4 cup mint leaves
- For a sweeter version, add liquid stevia or raw agave nectar

CHIA SEED RECIPES

Called the "Dieter's Dream Food," chia seeds are getting a lot of recognition lately through TV, newspapers, magazines, etc., and it's not because they make cute little animal-shaped plants (although that is cool!). Chia seeds are being praised for many things including their fantastic nutrient profile, which proudly boasts iron, boron, essential fatty acids, fiber, and more. From claims that they may improve heart health to reducing blood pressure to stabilizing blood sugar to helping people lose weight to giving extra stamina and energy, these little guys have it going on!

To purchase chia seeds, visit KristensRaw.com/store.

CHIA FRESCA BREEZE I

Yield 1 serving

    2 teaspoons chia seeds
    1 cup water
    Juice of 1 orange
    2 teaspoons raw agave nectar
    pinch cinnamon

Stir all of the ingredients together in your favorite drinking glass and enjoy. I like drinking this with my glass straw so I can stir the beverage between sips to prevent the chia seeds from all settling in the bottom of the glass.

CHIA FRESCA BREEZE II

Yield 1 serving

2 teaspoons chia seeds

1 cup water

1 tablespoon fresh lemon juice

2 teaspoons raw agave nectar

pinch cayenne pepper

Stir all of the ingredients together in your favorite drinking glass and enjoy. I like drinking this with my glass straw so I can stir the beverage between sips to prevent the chia seeds from all settling in the bottom of the glass.

CHIA FRESCA BREEZE III

Yield 1 serving

2 teaspoons chia seeds

1 cup water

Juice of 1/2 grapefruit

2 teaspoons raw agave nectar

dash powdered ginger

Stir all of the ingredients together in your favorite drinking glass and enjoy. I like drinking this with my glass straw so I can stir the beverage between sips to prevent the chia seeds from all settling in the bottom of the glass.

CHAPTER 6

WINE DRINKS

DID SOMEBODY SAY DRINKS?

While I understand that alcohol destroys pretty much every cell it comes in contact with, I also understand that not everyone is going to swear off alcohol for life.

If you would like to spice things up with a little alcohol, wine is your best choice. Not only does it blend well with many delicious ingredients, it's also Raw, unlike beer or distilled spirits. Look for *organic* and *vegan* wine, too.

The following drinks have a small amount of alcohol in them, which of course, you can alter to your preferences. Please remember that many people living the Raw lifestyle have very clean, efficient bodies that may respond to alcohol a little more strongly than normal. So if you've just started on the Raw lifestyle and don't drink often, be sure to start with just a small amount and see what happens. It may be all that you'll want for the evening. And, of course, don't drink and drive (you're smarter than that, I know).

Now with all the disclaimers aside, it's time to *HAVE SOME FUN!* I've included some awesome, classy and sexy cocktails for you to enjoy.

* Note that all of the following beverages can certainly be made "virgin" (without alcohol) so be sure to try them like that as well. They are *GOOD!*

Treat yourself! Make sure to serve these in your fine wine goblets or wine glasses.

SASSY STRAWBERRY APERITIF

See photo at KristensRaw.com/photos.

Yield 2 servings

One of my favorites, and it's so pretty, too.

1/4 cup white wine

1/2 cucumber, peeled and chopped

2/3 cup strawberries, stemmed and chopped

2 tablespoons raw agave nectar

2 tablespoons goji berries

pinch nutmeg

1 cup ice

Blend all of the ingredients, except the ice, until smooth. Add the ice and blend to desired texture.

GRANNY MAC POTENT LIFE

Yields 2 servings

Oh boy... this one is really good. You might end up drinking it all yourself.

1/4 cup macadamia nuts

(continued)

1/4 cup white wine

2 Granny Smith apples, cored and chopped

1 kiwi fruit, peeled and chopped

1/2 cup strawberries, stemmed and chopped

1/4 inch fresh ginger, peeled and chopped

2 tablespoons raw agave nectar

1/2 cup water or more if needed

Grind the macadamia nuts in a dry blender. Add the remaining ingredients and blend until creamy, adding water until you achieve your desired consistency.

BLUEBERRY EYES COOLER

Yield 2 servings

Delicious, refreshing and fun.

1/4 cup white wine

2 apples, cored and chopped

1/2 cup blueberries

2 tablespoons fresh lemon juice

1 cup ice

Blend all of the ingredients, except the ice, until smooth. Add the ice and pulse to chop.

VANILLA LOVE CLOVE

Yields 2 servings

Elegant and F-A-B-U-L-O-U-S.

1/4 cup white wine

2 cloves, crushed*

2 bananas, peeled and chopped

1 cup *Raw Nut/Seed Milk* (see recipe, p. 25)

1 - 2 tablespoons raw agave nectar (start with 1 tablespoon and add more as desired)

1/2 teaspoon vanilla extract

1 cup ice

Blend all of the ingredients in a blender until smooth, adding more water to get your desired consistency.

* You can find cloves in the spice aisle of your local health food store.